NEVER

A Book of Daily DON'TS
for Personal
Happiness & Success

MICHAEL LEVINE

PHOENIX
BOOKS

Copyright ©2006 Michael Levine and Phoenix Books and Audio Inc.

ISBN: 1-59777-531-2

Library of Congress Cataloging-In-Publication Data Available

Cover and Book Design by: Sonia Fiore

Printed in the United States of America

Phoenix Books
9465 Wilshire Boulevard, Suite 315
Beverly Hills, CA 90212

10 9 8 7 6 5 4 3 2 1

Whenever we are directed not to do something, we invariably want to. Long ago in the Garden of Eden, the first humans couldn't even follow a simple admonition: "Never eat from the tree of good and evil." This first encounter with a "Never" is a prime example of simple rules that parents make to keep children from hurting themselves in their independent explorations of life. Nevertheless, the allure of forbidden fruit, made more enticing by the promise of secret knowledge, was an irresistible combination.

Adam and Eve ate that apple and our teeth are still hurting.

Human beings are born into the world as wonders, full of potential and hope. We are generally happy creations, albeit a little selfish. The trouble we have in life revolves around not doing the things we should and doing the things we shouldn't. Effort and restraint bring order to our lives and allow us to enjoy the fruits of our labors.

Most people think of rules as laws and those who enforce those laws (policemen, clergy, parents, teachers, etc.) as people who invade our private boundaries and keep us "in check." You don't speed because there is the increased risk of a serious accident if you do. You don't run a red light because you also could be involved in an accident. But the red light was put there to regulate traffic and give everyone else a turn to use the street to avoid confusion. The same holds true when our parents and teachers told us not to talk when someone else was talking. That restraint allows everyone to have a turn to speak and to be heard. Somehow, though, we forget that rules are good things and breaking them must be done with the utmost intention and full knowledge of the consequences, not just because we want to slide through life, hedonistically doing whatever we want, whenever we want, no matter who it harms.

Today, to find contentment in the flurry of activity we call living, we need to be more mindful of how we live. Bill Moyers says in Creation: A Living Conversation, "So the beginning of knowledge could well be prohibition, boundary, limit". It is important to listen to counsel not to do things that will cause us pain and stress.

That's why I've written this little book. If we did nothing more than follow these admonitions, we have a pretty good guide to happiness and success in life. The underlying foundation of these guides is abstinence – not doing something – and, therefore, they require some discipline from us.

But the following "Nevers" are not burdensome. The advice the "Nevers" give is easy to incorporate into our daily activities. These "Nevers" are little acts that we can do to show kindness and value to other human beings. Some of the

"Nevers" may even bring a smile to our lips because of their fresh views of human nature. They offer a simple perspective that can help us view life and our relationships with others in new and improved ways.

Michael Levine
Los Angeles, California

Dedication

The book is dedicated with immense gratitude to M. Scott Peck, M.D., my teacher, healer and minister to the day he died and beyond.

Acknowledgements

Special thanks to Michael Viner and his outstanding team at Phoenix Books including Sonia Fiore, Julie McCarron and Sal Preciado.

A special note of gratitude to the President of LCO, Dawn Miller for her extraordinary contributions to our company and it's continued growth.

My LCO-Levine Communications Office team Lorena Alamillo, Liam Collopy, Donna Dillard, Ali Duncan, Lauren Lewis, Patricia Mora, Jackie Noh, Collin Pike.

My special friends, without whom my life would be significantly less full: Peter Bart, Craig Black, Adama Christing, Rick Citron, Craig Hollander, Richard Imprescia, Karen Karsian, Phil Kass, Tara Keenan, Dr. Robert Kotler, Nancy Mager, John McKillop, Mark Miller, Evadne Morakis, Craig Nelson, Cable Neuhaus, Alyse Reynolds, Steve Shapiro, David Weiss, Lisa Yukelson.

Never

confuse the
commandment
to honor your
parents with
loving them.

Never

buy a

cheap

parachute.

Never forget that if people concentrated on the really important things in life, there would be a shortage of fishing poles.

Never overlook that the problem with the rat race is that even if you win, you're still a rat.

Never

sleep with
your eyes open.

Never

drink the water
in Mexico.

Never

forget that
every exit is
an entry to
somewhere else.

Never

dive into
an empty pool.

Never

think about
the weekend
on Monday.

Never

sacrifice
your beliefs,
goals,
values,
or morals.

Never exchange
your integrity
for success.

Never try to run
before you can walk.

Never
forget to put
yourself in
others' shoes
once in a while.

Never
laugh when
someone
is crying.

Never

eat yellow snow.

Never

walk into a communal bathroom without shoes on.

Never see the glass as half empty.

Never pass up chocolate.

Never

stop dreaming.

Never

trust everyone.

Never
tell your
teacher the
dog ate your
homework.

Never
forget life
is short.

Never
forget life
is difficult.

Never

expect to have anything
just handed to you.

Never

just give 100%.

Never

forget to listen
to your conscience.

Never

confront a postal
worker during
the holidays.

Never

leave your telephone
ringer on after a
"heavy" night.

Never

overlook that the most
well-meaning advice won't
amount to a hill of beans
if you're not addressing
the real problem.

Never

take an
anorexic to an
"all-you-can-eat"
buffet.

Never

call a sports
fanatic during
the Super Bowl.

Never

cut in front
of a pregnant woman
in a fast food
restaurant.

Never

take a nymphomaniac
to a strip club.

Never

become the one that says
"Turn that music down!"

Never

forget that
when you
feel far away
from God,
it is you
who moved,
not God.

Never humiliate your spouse.

Never humiliate your children.

Never

forget that children, marriage, and parenthood are God's plea with the human race to grow up.

Never

try to tell Babe Ruth how to hold the bat.

Never
believe a good mother
can be a good father.

Never
believe that a good father
can be a good mother.

Never
say "Big Time."

Never
lose your sense
of healthy shame.

Never

let anyone hear you
impersonate Marvin Gaye
singing "Let's Get it On."

Never

expect a woman
to pick up a check.

Never

miss a
Bruce Springsteen
concert.

Never

underestimate
the Village
People.

Never

listen to rap
music when
you're stressed.

Never

forget the law
of the harvest:
no planting,
  no harvesting.

Never

believe that talk show callers accurately represent talk show listeners.

Never

believe that people
are basically good.

Never

fail to send a
thank-you note after
a job interview.

Never

create cheap
drama at work;
your job is
to make your
boss's life easier.

Never

forget that gifts
are not enough
and bullion is not
enough; character
is the only
real gold.

Never

marry someone
you wouldn't
choose as
your best friend.

Never
ask if it
was good
for you.

Never
accept PMS
as an excuse.

Never

ask if she is expecting.

Never

forget that
psychosomatic illnesses
are often reincarnations
of cumulative resentment,
deep disappointment,
and disillusionment.

Never

overlook that
the Bible talks more
about wealth and money
than any other topic.

Never

think **life** is fair.

Never

Never spend more time
watching TV
than reading.

Never

think your teacher is tough;
wait until you get a boss
who doesn't have tenure.

Never

think flipping burgers is beneath your dignity; your grandparents had a different word for burger-flipping—they called it opportunity.

Never

forget that life is not
divided into semesters;
in real life you don't
get summers off.

Never

forget to be nice to
nerds because chances
are you'll end up
working for one.

Never

comb your hair
over anything except
more hair.

Never

assume other people
want to see you
in shorts.

Never
try to define love.

Never

forget that people are
where they are because
of who they are.

Never

leave the last cookie on the plate.

Never

make a chair out of a cactus.

Never
nickname your
child Sparky.

Never
chew gum while
giving a speech.

Never

wait in a doctor's
waiting room longer than
half an hour.

Never
date your friends' ex-lovers.

Never
let a small argument
ruin a friendship.

Never

put your car keys down "just for
a minute" in the trunk of your car.

Never

treat people other than
how you like to be treated.

Never

forget how fragile your life is.

Never

eat cookies
left for Santa.

Never

tell a pun and wonder
why no one laughed.

Never

tell someone you
will call them and
then don't.

Never
stand someone
up on a date.

Never
act like someone
you are not.

Never

drive slower than
everyone else
on the freeway.

Never

try to put
your foot in
your mouth.

Never

try to wise up
a chump.

Never

roll up the sleeves
of a T-shirt.

Never

wear white shoes
after Labor Day.

March 7

Never

stick your tongue

to a flagpole in

the middle

of winter.

Never
drive if you are sleepy.

Never
hold yourself back
from crying.

Never

eat before going
on a roller coaster.

Never

wear a white dress
while eating spaghetti.

March 11

Never

wear a thong if you
weigh more than 300 pounds.

Never

name your son Yehuda, Dick
or any other name that will
get his ass kicked.

Never
forget to wear a bra
when it's raining.

Never

expect favors to be returned.

Never

assume you are being listened to.

Never

walk with
your head down
(you don't know
what you'll miss).

Never

refer to yourself in the third person.

Never
repeat yourself
unnecessarily.

Never
forget where
you came from.

Never

tell the same story to the same person twice.

Never

talk to yourself out loud.

Never

drink beer claiming
that the barley
and hops are
for roughage.

Never

mistake
intelligence
for wisdom.

Never

Never skip breakfast.

Never

compete against someone
whose life depends on
the outcome.

Never
ask a question,
if unprepared
for an answer.

Never
call every friend
your best friend.

Never

give someone more
than three chances.

Never

waste your time telling
a member of the flat
earth society that the
earth is round.

Never

debate
William F.
Buckley.

Never

underestimate
the government's
ability to screw
things up.

Never
fall asleep
at a bar.

Never
believe conspiracy
theories about
bureaucracies.

Never

transfer a caller
that you can
help yourself.

Never

miss an opportunity
to compliment your
friends, family,
and lovers.

Never

refer to it as pre-marital sex if you're not planning on getting married.

Never
beg for love.

Never
take a long trip
without checking
the tire pressure.

Never

ask someone working
for you to give you
a sponge bath.

Never

wear white socks
with black shoes.

Never

underestimate the
change in your life
a child will bring.

Never

assume an airplane
will be on time.

Never
make enemies
with your banker.

Never
lie to your attorney.

Never

cheat your
tax preparer.

Never

fail to accept
constructive
criticism.

Never

count your calories
more carefully than
your blessings.

Never

make the most important ques-
tion at your wedding, "Should
we serve chicken or fish?"

Never

shake hands with someone
if you have a cold.

Never

tell a young boy that
wrestling is fake.

Never
underestimate
God's power.

Never

overestimate

your power.

Never

believe idiots.

Never

miss an opportunity to feel sorry for Michael Jackson.

Never

forget the
power of saving
and investing.

Never

forget what
a tough job
the police have.

Never

fail to apologize
when you make
a mistake.

Never

underestimate the
capacity of another
person to have the same
shortcomings as you.

Never
waste food.

Never
waste your life.

Never

admire people you
wouldn't trust to
baby-sit your children.

Never

fail to give credit to
those who helped shape you.

Never

display your loyalty to
The Flinstones by yelling
out "Yabba-dabba-doo!"

Never

ask your elderly mother how she
is feeling, unless your schedule
is open for the next hour.

Never

let the IRS push you around.

Never

forget the IRS works for you.

Never

try to describe the taste
of an artichoke to someone
who has never eaten one.

April 20

Never

forget that every heart
surgeon can't be the best.

Never

think that heaven is
reserved for you.

Never
forget that people
respect wisdom
but obey pain.

Never

lose sight of the fact
that America is the only
nation on Earth with the
immigration problem of too
many people wanting in.

Never
automatically
dismiss
stereotypes.

Never
underestimate silence.

Never
talk on a
cell phone in
a restaurant.

Never

knock down
someone's sandcastle.

Never

confuse people
and animals.

Never

believe conspiracy
theories.

Never

eat fruit without
thinking of who
planted the tree.

Never

believe there's no
evil in the world.

Never

forget the
lesson taught.

Never

forget to stretch
before and
after exercising.

Never

forget to be
cautious about the
word "impossible."

Never

put down Vietnam vets.

Never

underestimate
The Three Stooges.

Never

underestimate
Jack Benny.

Never

spend your money
before you have it.

Never

use righteous
indignation to mask
your own stupidity.

Never put off until tomorrow what you can do today.

Never trouble another for what you can do yourself.

Never overlook
that a strong
part of sexuality
is making members
of the opposite
sex feel good
about themselves.

Never

forget that you
don't see things as
they are; you see
things as we are.

Never

fail to prepare for
a torturous experience
when flying on
commercial airlines.

Never

compare baseball to poetry.

Never

buy discount toilet paper.

May 12

Never pad your resume.

Never underestimate gratitude.

Never

call the waiter a nickname.

Never

break up with someone
over the telephone.

Never date someone with a swastika armband.

Never smell

old sneakers.

Never

pick your nose
in public.

Never

defend Clinton's
misconduct.

Never

forget that all men
have Clinton's
instinct with women.

Never

close your eyes for
30 seconds and say
"Ahhh..." while sitting in
a hot tub with strangers.

Never

run for a bus—there will
always be another.

Never
forget your sunglasses
on a sunny day.

Never

refer to your cats
as "furry children."

Never

drop change in a tip jar
to impress someone.

Never

smoke and jog.

Never

let school
interfere
with your
education.

Never
pray for
a sports
team to win.

Never

stop learning.

Never

fail to return
a lost wallet.

Never

believe that a
condom will protect
your heart.

Never
kiss and tell.

Never
accept a gift without
saying "thank you."

Never
let your kids fail to say
"please" and "thank you."

Never

wear a baseball
cap backwards.

Never

believe a
car salesman.

Never

believe a
security guard
will protect you.

Never
teach
children
that
all lying
is wrong.

Never
burn a
bridge
with an
old employer.

Never
give your lover's
genitals a nickname.

Never

use "I didn't know what
to say" as an excuse.

Never

fail to acknowledge
a personal letter.

Never
date anyone who
didn't like *Annie Hall*.

Never
kiss someone right
after eating chili.

Never

consider someone who
cheats a friend.

Never

ask a woman if she had a boob job.

Never

ask a Mormon missionary
if he wants to chat.

Never

give murderers a second chance.

Never

underestimate the ability of airlines to mistreat you.

Never

forget that you are
what you think.

Never

try to get by
on a smile.

Never

offer pork to a rabbi.

Never

offer food to a supermodel.

Never

assume a computer
will work.

Never

assume a cell phone
will work.

Never

try to

impersonate

Austin Powers.

Never

wear

sunglasses

indoors.

Never

speak French
with a broken accent.

Never

miss an opportunity to
see the leaves change
color in the fall.

Never

go on a date and afterwards ask the person if they want a rematch.

Never

forget unity
requires unanimity.

Never

forget to honor
Martin Luther King.

Never

believe all tall guys
play basketball.

Never

forget everyone has
some addiction.

Never

forget that we are all
frauds and hypocrites.

Never

forget that business
is about making things
and selling things.

Never

underestimate the
similarities between Judaism
and Christianity.

Never

deny the power
of Elvis.

Never ask
to borrow anything that
you know will look
better on you.

Never forget

that your friends want to know when they have food in their teeth.

Never

discuss salaries.

Don't go there. Period.

Never

conclude that the
grandest intention is more
valuable than the tiniest
accomplishments.

Never

drive with your
turn signal on.

Never

steal someone's
babysitter.

Never

apologize by leaving a
message on an answering
machine or sending
an e-mail.

Never

forget to dry-clean borrowed clothes before giving them back.

Never

test the depth of
water with both feet.

Never

walk barefoot in
the yard at night.

Never

think if you lend
someone $20 and never
see them again, that it
wasn't worth it.

Never

forget that some days
you are the bug and
some days you are
the windshield.

Never

ask a police officer,
"Are you from the
Village People?"

Never

forget that if at first you don't succeed, sky diving is not for you.

Never

forget that good judgment
comes from bad experiences,
and a lot of that comes
from bad judgment.

Never
miss a good chance
to shut up.

Never
assume that empathy
equals sympathy.

Never
put pot in your
boss's brownies.

Never
chew gum during
a job interview.

Never

think a successful
cartoon will make
a good movie.

Never
add ketchup
to your iced-tea.

Never
weigh yourself
with wet hair.

Never

pick your teeth with
a dollar bill at
the dinner table.

Never

eat chili
for breakfast.

Never

take a job for 16
hours at a low rate.

Never

fail to stand for
something or else you'll
fall for anything.

Never

continue to dig when
you're in a hole.

Never

fail to realize that all
journeys begin internally.

Never

fail to define a goal,
or someone else will
do it for you.

Never

get married already
thinking that you'll
probably end up divorced.

Never
give your phone
number out
to strangers.

Never
confuse suntan lotion
with mayonnaise when you
are making a sandwich.

Never
think of a
swimming pool and a bath
as the same thing.

Never

cook food you
can't pronounce.

Never

pass up the
opportunity to
pet a dog.

Never

trust a surgeon
who constantly hums
"The thigh bone's
connected to the
hip bone."

Never

pass up the chance
to read to a child.

Never
run a red light.

Never
confuse lust for love.

Never

confuse like for love.

Never

believe that in relationships, fights about mayonnaise are always about mayonnaise.

Never

argue with your hairstylist (especially when your hair is being cut or colored).

Never

pee in the pool.

Never

do "Nevers" at a social dinner/gathering.

Never

yell at your proctologist.

Never
jump to rash
conclusions.

Never
be too stubborn to
ask for directions.

Never

be afraid to get lost.

Never

answer questions with
"Because I said so."

Never
refer to public
property as yours.

Never
use big words
if unsure of
their meaning.

Never
state the obvious.

Never
forget to call
the next day.

Never

honk for no reason.

Never

expect to win if you don't play.

Never
hold your breath

for fun

(you'll want that breath later).

Never

videotape sexual acts.

Never

criticize a job
you couldn't do better.

Never
refer to the
"good ol' days."

Never
say something's
"good enough."

Never

forget that deception
is a soldier's most
potent weapon.

Never

forget growth is messy.

Never

misdirect anger.

Never

underestimate children.

August 4

Never

call into pre-recorded
talk shows.

Never

run to the bathroom
(it makes it obvious).

Never

focus on regret.

Never

talk to

inanimate objects.

Never

expect to wait

"just a second."

Never

consult a psychic.

Never

throw away good food.

Never

try to live through
your children.

Never
believe that there were no
arts before federal funding.

Never
believe the business of
creating oppression is the
government's great prosperity.

Never

hire the television
as a babysitter.

Never

lobby against the N.R.A.
(they have guns).

Never

refer to your car as "she."

Never

take your cell phone

to church.

Never believe that

taxes are too low but ATM

fees are too high.

Never

ask a woman if it's
"that time of the month."

Never

ask "what's wrong"
more than once.

Never

lose touch
with old friends.

Never
be late
without calling.

Never

mispronounce words in
a foreign language
(you don't know what they mean).

Never

give your child the same
name as a celebrity.

Never

believe that the same
teacher who can't teach
fourth-graders how to read
is somehow qualified
to teach those same kids
about sex.

Never

pass someone else's
story off as yours.

Never

expect respect
without giving it.

Never

cheat on a lover with one of their friends.

Never
start a sentence with
"Uhhhh..."

Never

think you're the
only one with a
friend named Smitty.

Never

forget that a person
who is nice to you but
rude to the waiter is
not a nice person.

Never

be unwilling
to compromise.

Never

argue with Little
League umpires.

Never

scratch on
the eight-ball.

Never

double-down without looking
at the dealer's hand.

Never

table feed your dog.

Never

take pictures
at a bachelor party.

Never

order Italian food
at a steakhouse.

Never
take advantage
of a privilege.

Never

blame the referees.

Never

count how many
beers you drank.

Never

buy cheap liquor.

Never

believe that guns
in the hands of
law-abiding Americans
are more of a threat than
U.S. nuclear weapons
technology in the hands of
Chinese Communists.

Never

call a flight attendant

"stewardess."

Never

take a sunny day for granted.

Never

underestimate the
healing power of time.

Never ask
your date if he or she's
"gonna eat that."

Never forget
that tomorrow is
another day.

Never feel
obligated to agree.

Never

forget to wash
your hands after
using the restroom.

Never

take out the
fortune before you
eat the cookie.

Never

wear granny
underwear with
tight pants.

Never

mix vodka with tequila.

Never,

under any circumstances take a sleeping pill and a laxative on the same night.

Never

wear pantyhose

with open-toed shoes.

Never

go to the gym
if you have gas.

Never

lick a steak knife.

Never

use your Mastercard to
pay off your Visa bill.

Never vandalize police property while on television.

Never stay silent while a friend is being abused.

Never

put a loved one in a
retirement home without
visiting them.

Never

watch *The Blair Witch Project*

without taking a

motion-sickness pill.

Never

wear gang colors

to a gun show.

Never

use a hatchet to

remove a fly from a

friend's forehead.

Never

answer the question,
"Honey, do I look fat?"

September 19

Never put "Exhibitionist" under "Additional Skills" on a job application.

Never include Hamburger Helper in a Valentine's Day gift basket.

Never

interrupt a prostate exam
by requesting that he dim
the lights and put on a
Johnny Mathis CD.

Never

forget that the cobra
will bite you, whether
you call it
a cobra or Mr. Cobra.

Never

re-give a gift.

Never
cease advancing
confidently in the
direction of
your dreams.

Never

forget the
"Tiffany Theory."

Never

confuse your career
with your life.

Never

confuse wealth

with success.

Never

talk under

your breath.

Never

substitute sugar with salt.

Never
be afraid
to laugh at
yourself.

Never
jump on
the bandwagon.

Never

form an opinion
out of apathy.

Never

ignore the difference
between thinking
something and saying it.

Never

confuse spirituality
with religion.

Never

overlook water
as your cheapest
medicine.

Never

go to bed with
curlers
in your hair.

Never

assume that others
will be enamored of your
pets, children, or
singing voice.

Never

ask your mother what she
thinks of your nose-ring.

Never ask your father if you should get a summer job.

Never go on the road without duct tape.

Never eat broccoli or beans before a road trip.

Never try to out-drink a bar breathalyzer machine. There's a reason why it only registers.08.

Never

talk to a bore without
an excuse to leave.

Never

sing with

headphones on.

Never

do your taxes in pen
the first time.

Never

paint your living
room black.

Never

do crossword puzzles in ink.

Never
buy cheap mayonnaise.

Never

worry if the glass is
half-full or half-empty;
be thankful you have a glass
and there's something in it.

Never
do your nails
while driving on
the interstate.

Never

buy more souvenirs
than you can dust.

Never

count your newborn guppies
until you remove their
mother from the tank.

Never

buy food your cat hates
even if it's on sale.

Never

look for someone to
give you a clear and
compelling reason why
we observe daylight
savings time.

Never

put your car on cruise
control during rush hour.

October 20

Never

drink beer or milk

at room temperature.

Never

leave your car in the
snow during a snowstorm.

Never

tell someone they can't succeed. They might believe you and stop trying.

Never gamble with more than you have.

Never

fail to realize that
the world around us is
simply a mirror of thoughts,
feelings, and emotions.

Never pass the police car.

Never
say bad things
about good people.

Never
cook bacon naked.

Never
look prettier
than
the bride.

Never
put your cat in
the microwave.

Never

kiss with your eyes open.

Never

take old wives' tales
seriously (unless you're
married to one).

Never

buy a secondhand
parrot.

Never

ask for a doggy bag
at a buffet.

Never

believe anyone when
they say it will
only hurt a little.

Never

use a jackhammer
when a fly-swatter
will do.

Never
sell yourself short.

Never

ask "Why?" when
someone turns you
down for a date.

Never

compromise yourself
or your values for
a relationship.

Never

build walls around
your heart.

Never
wear socks with
high-heeled shoes.

Never
coordinate the color
of your make-up with the
color of your clothes.

Never

mistake a fat woman
for a pregnant woman.

Never

love someone
you don't like.

Never

blame others for
your mistakes.

Never

forget to take
responsibility for
yourself and for
your actions.

Never

name a child after candy,
days of the week, feelings
or abstract notions.

Never

come between a man
and his tools.

Never

eat yogurt without checking the expiration date.

Never
date out of your species.

Never
fail to acknowledge
the accomplishments
of a child.

Never

turn down
an invitation
to have tea
with the Queen.

Never

fail to return
a phone call.

Never

cut out articles in
a newspaper or
magazine until everyone
in the house has
read the publication.

Never
insult the cook.

Never

go out on a date alone.

Never

marry on the first date.

Never
"park" drunk:

accidents can happen.

Never

sign a bank contract.

Never

marry for money.

Never

misquote

Winston Churchill.

Never

pet a cat that's on fire.

Never

trust a naked bus driver.

Never tell a man you have already heard the joke he is preparing to amuse you with.

Never

neglect the

Salvation Army kettles

during holidays.

Never

watch *The Exorcist*
or *Psycho* alone.

Never

dot your i's with
hearts or smiley faces.

Never
take opportunities
for granted.

Never
race to a red light.

Never

take dieting advice
from an overweight person.

Never

sing along with
commercial jingles.

Never

murder.

Never

count out the underdog.

Never

answer defensively.

Never

fall victim to denial.

Never

count your casino
winnings until you
have cashed out.

Never

ask "What if..."

Never
slouch.

Never

bite your
fingernails.

Never

sit on the edge
of your seat.

Never
be afraid to
ask for help.

Never
try to fully
understand the
opposite sex.

Never
trust technology.

Never

think there's
anything wrong
with being skeptical.

Never

run with scissors.

Never

answer a
rhetorical
question.

Never

allow yourself to
channel-surf all
the way around
more than twice.

Never

participate in the
"Running of the Bulls."

Never

deny that you've thought about most of the things that Howard Stern says.

Never
drink to cure
a hangover.

Never
stand in
front of a
revolving door.

Never

leave your windows
open during a storm.

Never

forget that there is
always someone more and
less fortunate than you.

Never

allow a non-verbal
reaction speak louder
than your words.

Never
use a wet towel.

Never
fall asleep during sunbathing.

Never

leave an empty roll
of toilet paper.

Never

forget your umbrella.

Never

make the same
mistake twice.

Never

eat before running.

Never

dominate a conversation
with your life's details.

Never

look a gift horse
in the mouth.

Never

piss into the wind.

Never

break the rules
until you know them.

Never

settle for
second best.

Never

stop questioning.

Never

believe that information
is transformation.

Never

try to logically explain
to another your
fascination with S & M.

Never

play tug-of-war
with barbed wire.

Never
drink hot coffee
through a straw.

Never
hold back a sneeze.

Never

tell a fat woman
she has "such
a pretty face."

Never

tell a boy he can
jump off the roof
and float by holding
an open umbrella.

Never

file a frivolous lawsuit.

Never

blame society for
your failures.